Sisters

Sisters
Jennifer Copley

For Ron
with very best wishes
Jenny

Oct. '13

Published 2013 by
Smokestack Books
PO Box 408, Middlesbrough TS5 6WA
e-mail: info@smokestack-books.co.uk
www.smokestack-books.co.uk

Printed and bound in the U.K. by Martins,
Berwick upon Tweed.

ISBN 978-0-9575747-2-4

Middlesbrough
moving forward

Smokestack Books is represented
by Inpress Ltd
www.inpressbooks.co.uk

Acknowledgements

Acknowledgements are due to the editors of *The Rialto*, *Acumen*, *Flax* and the *Ware Competition Anthology* (2007) where some of these poems first appeared. 'Heart' won 2nd prize in the Ware Poetry Competition, 2009; 'There's a Graveyard near the Sea' won 2nd prize in the Yeovil Poetry Prize, 2009; 'Charity Walker' won 2nd prize in the Slipstream Poetry Prize, 2010; 'There's Another Graveyard' won 3rd prize in the Bridport Prize, 2010. I would like to thank Sue Harding, Kim Moore and Mike Barlow for their encouragement with this manuscript.

Contents

Repercussions

We didn't like the sound of *them*.
Aged five and six, we decided to disappear
before they got us so we made a hole
in the world and tumbled through.

It was dark in the beginning
but if we closed our eyes
it wasn't too different from being asleep.
We grew silver stars on our foreheads
so we could see each other.

Our food was sweet black earth.
Angels trimmed our hair.
They sewed on our buttons
and gave us vodka for colds.

The repercussions never found us.
Sometimes we hear their feet
but they walk right past
having no idea at all.

I

She Had Come So Far

since the petticoat race with her sister.
They'd set off at dusk, the arms
of their dresses tied round their waists,
jam sandwiches wrapped in a tea-cloth.
Her sister carried an apple pie in an old hat
which seeped through with a sugary smell
as they crossed the field.

They'd chatted together with no clue
where they were going. At least it wasn't cold
and when they split up at the forest edge,
she knew she would worry three things
around in her head: how to manage the dark,
how much jam there should have been
and had she left the jar in the right place
between the butter crock and spoons.

Sweet Tooth

When her tongue's dry,
she sucks a rhubarb stick.
It's sour without sugar,
catches her throat.

As she walks – her hair tucked
in her collar for comfort's sake –
she sends messages to her sister,
gets them back like a needle through the air.

In No Man's Land, she follows
small footprints through the mud.
They could be her sister's –
slightly pigeon-toed.

At night she dreams of a ladder –
her sister going up and down
delivering mint-creams
to their mother above the clouds.

Sundays

She and her sister have been sent to get blackberries.
Their legs are scratched, cardigans snagged.

They've just discovered a rabbit – no head, no throat.
Their father says dumb beasts don't go to heaven.
Man has dominion over them.

This morning the Kiwi smell of polished shoes:
his black boots, their grandmother's lace-ups,
two pairs of blue Mary-Janes.

That was their family, its hierarchy, spread out on the kitchen
    floor;
the shoe box containing two brushes for each colour –
a putting on and a taking off.
Each knowing what was expected of them.

Cliff

She and her sister stand at the top, looking down.
They can see the sea, the lighthouse
and the salt-walled church.

She and her sister think what it would be like to jump –
long hair, brown dresses,
tumbling into the giant water.

This morning they sat in church,
heard the story of the pillar of salt
and how Lot lay with his daughters.

She and her sister became aware of a shuddering
along the pew, a straightening of spines,
a pinkening of their father's ears.

Always they dread Sundays – the motherless day –
left to the will of God, the will of the wind.

Snow White & Rose Red

It's their favourite story
though they argue over who should get the prince.
Sometimes they see the bear-skin hearth-rug
twitch as if it wants something back.
Out of the dwarf's bad-tempered beard
they are knitting socks for their father
full of hidden brambles and burrs.

The Harlot

The talk in their house
is about the harlot come to live
at the end of the street.

She and her sister watch her nudge
through the stalls on market day
shaking her long red hair,
smiling at the men.

Mr. Proctor acts daft
when she buys some plaice.
Mr. Jenner blushes like one of his beetroots.
Old Sam mends her shoes for nothing.

Grandma says if she dares to enter church
there'll be ructions.
The sisters think this sounds like fun
compared to sermons and the long prayers.

Combing Her Sister's Hair

into sausage curls,
their mother's dress ready to step into,
lying on the bed like a beautiful ghost.

Twisting ivy into a coronet,
a scrap of Grandma's lace to make a veil.

She and her sister playing at weddings,
splashing their cheeks with rose water.

Watching themselves in the mirror.
One drowning in a long pale dress,
a curtain ring on her finger.
The other waiting her turn.

Bible

They're in trouble for resting a teacup
on top of the Bible – it's a crime
against the Holy Ghost.

Locked in their room,
they study the flyleaf:
John, died at sea, our only son
Eliza, taken from us, aged 2 years
Archie and Adelaide, stillborn…
A long list ending with their mother's name.

They dream she pushes her way
through the gilt-edged Indian paper,
the heavy black cover,
sits by their beds in the light of the moon.

Glass

She and her sister have three mirrors.
The first was Great Aunt Daphne's
which they share but the second,
silver-backed belonging to their mother,
they squabble over. The third, their father's
old shaving mirror, has two faces:
she prefers the one with double magnification
in which she can lose herself,
sink into a room she's never seen before.
Today they both stare into it, cheeks pressed together.
She can look right through the iris of her sister's eye.

The Swap

She and her sister have swapped bodies.
Yesterday, they cut their arms,
pressed them together.

She wakes with her face to the wall
on the wrong side of the bed.
She examines her breasts with amazement,
her little triangle of pubic hair.

She's taller, with unbitten nails.
As they walk to school,
she looks down on her old head
with the parting in the middle,
the cowlick on the crown.

Boys

Her sister has got a note
from a boy in their church.
He has long sweeping eyelashes
and the beginnings of a beard.
He lives in a nest like a bird.

She and her sister are going to meet
this boy (and his friend)
in the old shirt factory.
They plan to drop pebbles
along their route.

She and her sister have decided
they would quite like to kiss the boys
in the delicate part just under their wings.
They carry apples in their pockets
to lob through the window if need be.

Exchanging Information

Robert has bad breath,
James has a squinty eye.
There was no need for the apples
so they eat them, spitting out the pips
to see whose go furthest.
At home, their father shouts in the usual way.
He's wandering around in his vest,
the candlestick whiteness of his skin
looming suddenly from corners.

Dosed

with the Holy Ghost,
their father sprawls on the kitchen floor.
His mouth is all lopsided,
he can't move hand or foot.

Tugging and heaving,
she and her sister haul him
into their grandmother's dining-room bed,
tell neighbours he's gone to Scotland.

Now they have dominion,
it would make sense
to grind him away a little at a time
into their gravies and stews.

Harlots

was what he called them
in the days when he could speak.

Once, he took a knife,
tried to hack off their hair
but the postman's arrival
stopped him in his tracks.

Now they wear it half way down their backs –
a riot of loose curls.

Heart(s)

When they were children,
she and her sister each had a heart.
Now they share one, hold it
between them like their child.

Evenings, all three sit together
on the sofa reading novels.
The heart likes poetry
with a strong beat.

She and her sister prefer stories
of exploration in foreign climes,
the hero's shirt staying crisp
under difficulties.

Visitors

There were never afternoons
like the ones they had,
their father out of the way,
their knees together, podding peas,
top and tailing goosegogs,
letting the summer rain rinse them.

She and her sister didn't want visitors
but they pulled the moon
in through a sash window
squeezing him all out of shape,
his custard-coloured eyes popping.

Next they went for the sun, burning
the curtains, fusing the lights.
He sat in a ball on the sofa
chafing to be free, stuffing
the cushions with radiation.

She and her sister had the only illuminated
house in town. People went round
with lamps strapped to their foreheads,
pasty skinned and inarticulate.

Summer

The first sign it was going to be over
was the wind tearing down rose branches.

Her sister began to have a faraway look,
a leaning away look,

going out in secret, scuffing her footprints
so nobody could follow.

Given

Her mother, leaning over her cot.
A milky smell, a smell of skin,
the Dreft she can only identify now, years later.
The hurt she felt, like a nut in her heart.
A gate swinging shut.
A latchet she could never unloose.

Taken

She and her sister have parted.
The black-haired lad on the black and white horse
snatched her up, tucked her in front of him
and off they set.

She watched them ride to the end of the road,
her sister hanging on to the white mane,
fingers threaded through it.
Only the lad looked back.

Addict

I won't forget you, her sister said,

but the thing with the black-haired lad
petered out and she came back
breathing a different way.

At night their knuckles still touched
but she often crept out of the house
when she heard the clop of ponies,
smelt the smoke from campfires.

Waiting

Her sister stands in the frozen garden
looking up and down the road.
She's worn a hole by the gate
but all the black-haired lads
have grown into men.

The mouse-haired butcher and baker,
the blond-bearded candlestick maker,
knock on the door but get no reply.
Then there's the balding rag and bone man
who once got a kiss behind the hedge.

Staying Put

She and her sister don't go to the surface anymore.
They prefer to stay put.
They sing to each other and all the beetles and ants.
This is a way of forgetting.

One day they find an underground river,
purple as a shawl. They set their possessions upon it,
watch the small tufts float away.
She and her sister know they have run out of time.

Now

there is no more *us*.
She stares at the sea, the lighthouse
and the salt-walled church
it's too late to enter.

Everything is snapped shut
like the handbag their mother
always carried. They found it
nestled under the sheet that last day.

Her sister never used a handbag.

Rebekah

It is time to gather things in,
things that have been laid out ready.
She would rather stare at the fire.

She makes an apple pie but cannot eat it,
remembers the one they carried in a hat
the night they ran off,
leaving their father to polish shoes.

Mary and Martha, Leah and Rachel.
But who was Rebekah?
She cannot recall
but loves the name's old spelling.

Seashore

No one could ever make her sister
do anything she didn't want.
She'd stick out her bottom lip,
have to be dragged.

Now she's happy
just walking on the seashore of Heaven.
Black-haired lads have been left behind
in the silence of the earth.

Heaven is like a huge buttoned-up cushion.
They can't fall out.
Sometimes it's a little rough
along the seams.

They go about arm in arm. Their necks are long,
they can see over mountains.
Flowers grow in their hair – primroses, daisies;
the wild ones are the best.

II

Found

On the Stairs

On the first step, the hungriest one.

On the second, the bookish one, eyes wide open.

On the third, the one who carried water.

Those that were beautiful, on the fourth,

Those that were not, on the fifth.

The ones that came last, swept the others up.

Then they broke the brooms, made us pick up the splinters.

Down the Hall

Coats. An alarming number, all with hoods,

people stuffed in even if they didn't fit.

Their eyes were hidden but their hands

grew coarse dark hair.

Over their shoulders were bags – buckled, zippered,

velcroed – ones that snapped tight shut.

When they opened them up to show us

their travelling companions, we got out of there.

In the Dining-room

'a sea of troubles'.

We swam around choking with salt,

bumping up against the legs of chairs.

You had on your stiff upper lip

but your breaststroke was limp, your crawl, dodgy.

Chin up, you spluttered as we passed third time round.

When I looked again, you'd gone under.

Through the Patio Doors

our laburnum, buckled over,

spilling its beautiful yellow poison.

Where were you? I searched the bushes –

only a spade warm from your fingers,

the grass-box half-emptied,

next door's gardener lifting the clipping-shears.

Back Inside

the house had changed shape,

there were doors I didn't recognise

leading to cellars,

huge grey lanterns of dust,

wormwood and gall.

I followed the arrows (drawn shakily)

down to an underground stream and there you were.

No digging was required.

Between our Beds

when I laid you down,

a sudden invasion of cockroaches.

They waved their legs through the gloom.

I ran round collecting towels, a hair-dryer,

aluminium foil to warm you as you struggled.

Behind the Headboard

mistake after mistake.

I tried to gather them up.

The one who looked like an angel was slippery.

The one who cried remorselessly wouldn't be touched.

The other six bound themselves together. Dead weights.

Outside, starlings were flocking, wheeling together, a clean sweep

then burying themselves in trees by the gate.

Like the trees were the ones making those harsh cries,

opening the leaves of their throats in the dusk.

III

There's a Graveyard Near the Sea

where the dead are buried standing up.
When we go through the red brick
falling-down gateway, all we see are tussocks
but we know that beneath our feet
are fishermen and bakers,
shepherds and serving-maids,
children with the plague still on them.
Although they don't have to do anything
but stand there, the dead are weary of the upright position,
long to lie curled up amongst their fishing-nets
or bowls of dough. They beg us to dig down,
carve them out more space, break their legs if we have to,
pull the dirt from their ears so they may listen to the sea's music.

Doctor's Visit

He picks up her hand, lets it flop back,
tells her not to worry,
tells us she's had a stroke.

We've been trying to find things
in her cupboards – Germolene,
Zambuk, Slippery Elm.

There's no rhyme nor reason to her storage –
corn plasters next to tinned meat,
oranges in the bread bin.

There's a bottle of milk in the washing machine.
She's never found out how to work it
since we took away her old Servis
with the built-in mangle.

Bathtime

Not the last time she was ill but the time before that, she was
in the bath most of the day because it helped the pain. She
said she didn't mind if this was dying as long as she didn't
have to do it twice. We watched her flick hot water over her
white stomach, remembered when things were the other way
round; us in the bath always whining for more hot. If the
wind changes, she'd say, your faces will stick like that. When
she had her stroke, it was nothing to do with the stormy day
that drooped her eye and twisted her mouth to one side.

Buying Peace

We went to the hardware shop
but it was shut. Someone had the idea
of trying the haberdasher
which was where we found a single roll.
It'll suffice, said the woman.
Back home we shook out the shining stuff –
a heavenly silk with a silver thread.
Our mother clasped it to her.

After she died (painfully)
it would not get out of the house,
scrunched itself up when called a charlatan.
In church – at the communion rail,
kneeling on blue cushions,
sticking our necks over the oak rim –
we smelt its rankness
on the robes of the priest
and in the Book of Common Prayer.

Black Bag

She didn't want to go,
clung on to the sheet
though the men lifted her gently enough,

respectfully, into the black bag,
zipping it up while we watched her disappear;
first the long thin shanks

then the pendulous breasts and face.
A wisp of fly-away hair caught in the zip's teeth,
it was quite a job to free it.

Going down the steps to the car (bonnet
spattered with blossom from the cherry tree)
a muffled protest could be heard –

she wasn't dressed!
Couldn't they wait till she got her handbag!

Heart

When the heart
cracks like a cup
and we wonder whether to glue it
or throw it away,

we leave it on the draining-board
while we decide.
In the night, the heart gets cold
because of the draughty crack

and it shivers
the way we do, in bed alone.
There's a hole behind our ribs
we can't stuff with a hanky.

Our mothers would say –
leave a wound open, let air get to it,
it'll heal quicker –
but what do mothers know?

Mothers leave us before we are ready,
waving goodbye from the gate
in their coats and good gloves,
handbags snapped tight shut.

Charity Walker

A woman we do not know, is walking.
In her bag she carries a picture of God,
a piano, hypothermia, her mother's goulash,
eternity in a five strand necklace,
a foxhole, an eclipse, her duty,
her concentration, a pool of brackish water,
her heartbeat and his heartache
and an envelope addressed to the next place.

The strain on her shoulder muscles is great
but she'll keep walking until she has visited
every house where a woman lives.
We watch the back of her head grow smaller
until it is a dot on the flanks of our fell.
Soon she will reach the top, drop down
into the secret streets of mining villages
where daughters belong to their fathers.

Lin's Farm

We wander round the room that was hers,
touching powdery walls, the coverlet with the stain.
From the window we see the spot
where he burnt the cradle.

When they married, she was sixteen, he thirty.
She was light as a bird, it was snowing,
so he carried her back to the farm
and the old four-poster.

The mattress was lumpy but clean,
the linen sheets crisp as apples.
Jugs of jasmine pressed against iced-up windows.
He'd laid a fire but his fingers couldn't light it.

Lin, he called her, though her name was Jane.
She was only half his size; he wore a size 12 shoe.
He gave her everything, even the farm.
Folk said she bled him dry, that she could
push him over with one small hand.

Shadows

One day they came,
stood in the corners of the lounge
or sat in the chair next to hers.
They didn't interfere,
they were mute,
they stayed downstairs.

Things changed.
Now when she gets into bed,
they sweep from the ceiling
as if they've been clinging there all day
waiting for her to be tired.
Don't come so close, she begs.

The shadows have turned into people:
her sister, her mother,
her grandmother with a cage of canaries
which she swings about like incense,
nieces not yet born (she knows them
from their red hair).

When she reaches out
they shake their heads
as if she's doing something wrong
so she closes her eyes
but the barking of previously owned dogs
drives her to distraction.
The dachshund chews her shawl,
tries to get under the bedclothes.

Chickens

Soft evening rain
which no one said would fall,
is falling now on our old aunt
and the cardboard box
she sits in daily after tea.
In other respects she's rational –
puts out her washing on blowy days,
grows her own veg –
but her anxious yellow eyes remind us
of chickens she kept in the war.
She knows she hasn't long;
fears winter with more penetrating rain,
the sogginess of cardboard.

The Grannies

There was once a Nice Granny and a Nasty Granny. Nice Granny lived in a small thatched cottage on the edge of a wood. Nasty Granny lived in a whiskery old caravan with two jackdaws. You said she used their feathers in her spells but I told you not to be so silly. Nasty Granny was just nasty, she wasn't a witch.

We were made to go and see both Grannies equally so it was fair. Nice Granny beamed all over her sweet pink face when she saw us coming up the garden path. She had the chocolate biscuits ready. Nasty Granny frowned so her eyebrows met in the middle. She never had any biscuits to hide.

Nice Granny sat us down on her plump sofa and asked about our day. Her furniture was covered with photos of us or old brown ones of her husband Jim who was killed in the war fighting for England under the flag of truth. Nasty Granny's husband died walking under some scaffolding which hadn't been tied together properly.

Nice Granny was with us all the way through our teens, buying us our first transistor radios, china ponies, a subscription to 'Jackie' then later 'Musical Express'. Nasty Granny gave us needle-cases, shoe-cleaning outfits and once, a battered old inkwell *to share* which she said was an antique.

In 1972 Granny and Granny died within a month. Nice Granny went peacefully. We like to think Jim came to fetch her and they're together somewhere. Nasty Granny chose to stay with us. She pops out of wardrobes when we least expect it, turns bedroom door handles creakily at night before disappearing downstairs to sour the milk.

Two Suitcases

We carry our grandmother's bones
in an old suitcase, leather,
with a tag marked Granny.
As we stand at the bus stop,
her finger bones drum impatiently
on the worn lid.

It's the second suitcase
we've housed her in.
She hated the first – cardboard
with a rusty lock; wind whistled
through the nail holes.

We board the bus.
Her vertebrae don't like the way
they're slung in the luggage rack.
The longer we keep them,
the more crumbly they become.

When she died, the silence spooked us.
We were nervous of her bones
because they wouldn't speak.
Now we're back to normal –
her complaining about the damp
if the suitcase isn't on carpet;

us making the point that most bones
moulder in cemeteries with no one to care.

Precious Ones

When we were growing up, our grandmother said:
Precious ones, I have flattened the stairs so you may not fall;
hidden away the knives for fear you cut yourselves.
Here is your meat. I have minced it free from bones.

Thank you, precious grandmother, we replied,
pushing her into the cellar and locking it on her screams.
We were young with the big fat key of life in our mouths
     and oh! how heartily sick we were
of being patted on the back every time we coughed.

Mousehole in the Bathroom

Out of it squeezes our grandma, dusting
debris from her bosom, smoothing down her braid.
We're not sure why she's back,
the bathroom wasn't her favourite place,
too vast and windy with slippy lino,
the earthenware bath a struggle for her hip.

Here's her tin of Ashes of Roses, rusty now,
the talc gone solid. Here's her jar of soaps –
Gardenia, Palm & Olive, Smith's Cremolia
still in its wrapper. She cups Pink Lilac Morny
in her palm and sniffs.

The cat's in the airing cupboard again.
Either she can't see him or she doesn't mind.
She scans the shelves, her face a puzzled frown.
Where are her best Egyptian cotton sheets?
She used to make our beds so tight,
we had to lie like mummies.

Husbands

We went down to the sea
and married wolves.
We rode on their backs,
the white wings of our veils
streaming out, our dresses
trailing in the surf.
The wolves were brothers –
Mighty and King. We loved
their jewelled eyes,
their shaggy coats,
the way they warmed
the cold skin of our legs.
They gave us things –
a gull's skull with a scream
still in its beak, the eye of a whale,
a sailor's last message pricked out with a pin.
Protect us from Jonnie Mattinson, we begged,
and they licked our feet and pledged it.

Minnie

Her belly filling her apron,
Minnie bends to the scrubbing brush.
Our floors are thick with suds,
buckets with scum.
We're stuck upstairs listening to *that cough.*
There's a slap for our legs
if we try to come down.

We're scared to step on her lather.
My sister thinks Minnie's fingers
are really barbed-wire –
one day she'll catch us
and we'll never be able
to unhook our dresses.

I say when we're older
we won't mind Minnie so much.
She just might choke
on a pebble in a sandwich
and we'll hear her lungs over and over
trying to get it out.

Uncle Charles

Don't tease them, Charles, our mother said
but we loved his Indian stories
like the one about Grandfather John,
laid to rest in a summer-house in Bangalore,
the coffin perched across a stool and two chairs.
Uncle Charles said if no one was about,
he'd fire caps at it with his gun.

One night he saw his grandfather
heave his way through the lid,
walk about the garden, bones clanking.
Then there was the time he let us touch
his bayonet. We ran our fingers
up and down the blade, felt a crust of blood
from someone Uncle Charles had sliced in two.

Uncle Arthur

Sometimes I think of Uncle Arthur
when I meet a bad-tempered person.
He had a rowing boat on Windermere,
took us out in it if he'd a mind.

We were told to sit still, be quiet,
never touch the oars.
They creaked in their rowlocks
as if he was making a mistake.

Uncle Arthur was a bank manager and bell-ringer.
He only had one child, our cousin Joan.
I heard him say to Dad, one was enough;
how could he put his wife through that again.

*

Joan didn't like me or my sister.
Perhaps it was our long feathery names,
perhaps it was our twosomeness,
the way we bunched together, folding

and unfolding our secret lives like a map.
When we went out in the boat,
she stood on a rock and stared, pebble-eyed,
the lake wind lifting her hair.

*

In old age, Uncle Arthur went peculiar.
He had to move into St. Cuthbert's
where he wandered round with an Accounts Book,
interviewed the nurses for loans.

They took him to church on Sundays.
He loved the Liturgy
but threw his hymn book down
if the vicar tried anything modern.

When it rained, he hid in his room
and cried for the lake,
rocked back and forth
as if the water was inside him.

We Were Afraid of the Seamstress,

pins poking from her mouth.
Her name was Miss Strachen –
a Scottish Presbyterian –
scorn poured from her lips
when she saw us at the door.

Bridesmaids again?
You'll never be brides, either of you,
with those complexions and that hair!
And who chose this material?
It won't suit *you* and it won't suit *you* –
driving in the pins.

Minnie's Kitchen

After tea she'd sit in front of the fire,
knees apart, skirt hitched up.
You could see her knickers.

As cinders clinked through the grate
she'd criticise dead friends,
decrepit aunts who lingered on,
a drunken cousin recently passed over.

Her hymn book lay on the table,
bristling in its black cover.
The purple marker took you straight
to the *Death & Judgement* section.

Texts

From the day we were born
they were carved into us,
each day a little deeper.
Prayers at the table,
Instructions, Woe-betides.
Our shoulders sagged.

Once, I called my father a fool
and was locked in the cellar.
Ghosts lived behind the coal
and although I prayed
for every last thing to be forgiven
a swarm of them came out,
soot hanging from their hair.

I tried every text in the book.

Bread

At Aunty Pol's we always had brown bread –
she called it Beacon – malty with a hard crust.
We were forbidden to touch the bread-knife.
Passed down the family, it had a wicked blade;
sharpened to thinness on the cellar step.

Pol lived in Leeds where there were
all those murders. One dark winter day
as she sawed at the too-fresh loaf,
ice slithered over my heart.
Would I be one of those girls in a back-street
found under a ropeful of washing.

Barbara & Jeff in the Deep Dark Wood

Barbara isn't playing out today, her mother said
as I stood on the step and waited in the cold.
I tried to peer round but she blocked the doorway.
I thought I could see an inch of Barbara's skirt;
hear her nasal breathing.

I hid behind the wall and watched. Suddenly,
Barbara and Jeff appeared, pushed outside
by a huge hand, the door banged shut.
They had no coats. All hunched up, they set off
down the road, across the car park, into the wood.

It was getting dark but I could see them
dropping scraps of white as they went.
I picked up every bit and ate it.
Barbara didn't notice, too busy sniffling.
Jeff was wiping his glasses.

I found my way back home
by the beam of my usherette's torch.
Snow was falling, trees were knotting together
and a merry owl was sharpening his beak
but they let me pass.

Now, there's a picture of Barbara and Jeff
on every lamppost.
Their eyes watch me as I go to school.
If it's windy, their hair sticks up in fright
and they spread their arms like scarecrows.

What Made Us Scared on Bardsea Beach

That you were a long way from the shore

That we called and called

That the wind stopped our mouths

That we couldn't make you hear

That our breath hurt

That you hadn't seen the bore

That you *had* seen the bore and still kept on

That we couldn't have reached you even if we'd tried

That we had to do what we were told:

JUST STAY THERE!

There's Another Graveyard

far more overgrown, brambly at the edges.
Sheep step across the threshold
liking the taste of this grass.
Our grandmother brought us here.
It was like a jar of quietness with a lid of sky –
the only place where you never cried.
She'd crochet, sitting straight-backed
against the wall, while I hunted four-leafed clovers
and you made grass and dandelion pies.
They say there's no sound when someone crochets
but I can remember the rasp of wrinkled fingers
against wool, the sucking of teeth as a corner was turned.

IV

Doll's House

1: Sugar-pink

She and her sister live in a sugar-pink house
belonging to Mr. Armstrong. Every morning
he moves them to a different room.
Today they are in the kitchen, sitting
at the table; in front of each, a glued-down
bacon rasher on a little white plate.

She and her sister have hinged legs which bend neatly.
They cannot close their eyes or smile,
their wooden lips are dumb but they think to each other –
thoughts whizzing back and forth like racing cars.
Their ears are red with so much to-ing and fro-ing.
Much as they'd like to attack the bacon, they cannot.

Tomorrow she and her sister will be in the lounge.
They like it there – more comfortable chairs,
a radio, a clock with a kind face.
The crinkly orange paper in the grate is cheerful
though they cannot reach the tongs.

She and her sister have no idea what will happen
when Mr. Armstrong dies but they hope
they'll be in the lounge on that last day.
The bedroom is dirty (a mouse lives in the skirting)
and the bathroom has a noisy tap
which gives them a migraine.

2: Bathtub

She and her sister are worried.
Mr. Armstrong is filling the house with furniture –
four chests of drawers,
bolsters and comforters,
so many pots and pans the kitchen shelf is listing.

He has given them a baby.
They don't know what to do with it.
Since Mr. Armstrong dumped it in the bathtub
it just lies there under the dripping tap.

The bedroom mouse takes a look
but whether it bites the baby,
she and her sister cannot tell.
Mr. Armstrong is too busy to notice.
Lately, he's been unpredictable
and when he gets hold of them, it hurts.

3: Dream

Mr. Armstrong is trying to drown her
but because it's a dream, she's not worried;
studies his whiskered face through fizzing bubbles.

Through the water she can see the baby
manacled to the edge of the tub
with strands of sticky soap.
There's a crack across its crown.

4: A Proper Family

She and her sister are puzzled.
Mr. Armstrong has taped them to the sofa.
This hurts me more than it hurts you, he says,
wagging his finger at them.

The baby has been released from the bathtub.
It still has the crack on its head
but the sculpted curl on its brow is crisp and clear.
The baby has bright blue eyes, red lips
and a dot for a tummy-button.
She and her sister have become quite fond of it.

Their thoughts still whiz back and forth
(now with a nursery rhyme element
which they hope the baby picks up on).
They're used to the sticky tape by now, the lounge
is cozy and the hostile mouse has disappeared.
Mr. Armstrong hasn't picked them up for ages.

5: Disaster

She and her sister have had a shock.
Mr. Armstrong knocked the baby off the sofa
while putting in new carpets.
Its head has cracked right open,
nothing but air inside.

She and her sister fear the tape
may be employed none too gently.
They send tender messages
across the shag-pile but the baby's ears
are askew, can't hear a thing.